DATE DUE

SPENCER HAYWOOD

SLICK WATTS

SHAWN KEMP

LENNY WILKENS

FRED BROWN

GARY PAYTON

JACK SIKMA

NATE McMILLAN

VIN BAKER

DERRICK McKEY

SAM PERKINS

RASHARD LEWIS

CREATIVE ◆ EDUCATION
AARON FRISCH

Published by Creative Education, 123 South Broad Street, Mankato, MN 56001

Creative Education is an imprint of The Creative Company.

Design and Art Direction by Rita Marshall

Photos by Allsport, AP/Wide World, NBA Photos, SportsChrome

Library of Congress Cataloging-in-Publication Data

Frisch, Aaron. The history of the Seattle SuperSonics / by Aaron Frisch.

p. cm. – (Pro basketball today)   ISBN 1-58341-114-3   1. Seattle SuperSonics (Basketball team)–History–

Juvenile literature. [1. Seattle SuperSonics (Basketball team)–History. 2. Basketball–History.] I. Title. II. Series.

GV885.52.S4 F75 2001   796.323'64'09797772–dc21   00-047346

First Edition 9 8 7 6 5 4 3 2 1

SEATTLE, WASHINGTON,

IS A CITY KNOWN FOR ITS

LARGE AND IMPRESSIVE FEATURES. NEAR THE HEART

of the city stands the 607-foot Space Needle, one of the world's most

recognizable landmarks. Seattle's natural wonders are also big. These

include the snowcapped Mount Ranier to the southeast, the sprawling

forests that surround the metropolitan area, and the sparkling blue

water of Puget Sound.

Also known as a leader in the field of aircraft and spacecraft man-

ufacturing, Seattle is home to the Boeing Company, which builds some

of the world's largest jets. In 1967, Seattle added another high-flying

WALT HAZZARD

attraction—a team in the National Basketball Association (NBA).

Fittingly, the franchise was named in honor of the powerful jets built in

the city, becoming the Seattle SuperSonics.

{WINNING WITH WILKENS} The SuperSonics'

first season was a painful one. With a roster of rookies

and aging veterans, Seattle posted a 23–59 record.

Forward Walt Hazzard provided plenty of offensive

punch, but the Sonics seemed to lack leadership.

The first-year Sonics averaged 118 points per game—a team record that still stands.

Seattle solved that problem after the season by trading Hazzard to

the Atlanta Hawks for veteran guard Lenny Wilkens. The trade paid off

immediately. In 1968–69, Wilkens finished second in the NBA in assists

as Seattle improved its record by seven wins. Sonics general manager

Dick Vertlieb was so impressed by Wilkens's leadership that he asked

the guard to also serve as coach the next season.

VIN BAKER

Like Lenny
Wilkens,
Slick Watts
was an out-
standing
floor general.

SLICK WATTS

Wilkens accepted the position of player-coach and quickly proved that he could excel in both roles. His calm personality and intelligence made him a great coach, and his speed made him an All-Star player. That first season as coach marked the beginning of a new career for Wilkens. Decades later, he would set the league record for most coaching wins in NBA history. He would also be enshrined in the Hall of Fame as both a player and a coach.

In **1969–70**, center Bob Rule poured in a team-record 49 points in one game.

9

Under their young coach, the Sonics continued to improve. In 1971–72, Seattle posted its first winning record. Besides Wilkens, the main reason for the Sonics' success was an explosive young forward named Spencer Haywood, who finished fourth in the league in scoring.

"When Spencer was on, he could demoralize the other team singlehandedly," explained Sonics center Bob Rule. "He'd pull up from 25

BOB RULE

Shawn Kemp's offensive skills reminded the Sonics' faithful of Spencer Haywood.

SHAWN KEMP

feet and launch one [shot] after another into the rafters. Somehow the

ball would usually come down snap in the center of the basket."

With the Sonics on the rise, Wilkens decided to step

down as coach in 1972 and concentrate solely on playing.

He would not be playing for Seattle, however. In a shock-

ing move, the Sonics traded Wilkens to Cleveland for

young guard Butch Beard. Seattle fans were disappointed

to see him go, but Wilkens would be back.

{BIG BILL AND LITTLE SLICK} Without Wilkens leading the

way, the Sonics fell apart, plummeting to 26–56 the next season. To

right the ship, Seattle brought in former NBA star Bill Russell as head

coach in 1973. As a player, Russell had led the Boston Celtics to an

incredible 11 league championships.

In only his second season in Seattle, Russell guided the Sonics to a

SPENCER HAYWOOD

winning record and their first trip to the playoffs. Providing most of

Seattle's firepower that season were Haywood and guard Fred Brown,

whose long-range bombs earned him the nickname "Downtown Freddie

Brown." Both players averaged more than 21 points per game.

The real spark plug that drove the Sonics, though, was Don Watts,

better known to fans as "Slick." At a slim 6-foot-1, Watts was one of the league's smallest players. He was widely known, however, for his great

speed and quick hands—and the bright green headband he wore around

In **1976**, the
Sonics were
virtually
unbeatable
at home,
winning 29
straight
games there.

his bald head.

After arriving as a little-known free agent in 1973,

Watts quickly won over Seattle fans with his hustle.

Watts was a good player and a good person, devoting

much of his time to local charities. "In the 10 years of the

14   Sonics, I don't know of one player on a par with Slick Watts as far as

desire on the court and ability to make people happy," team owner Sam

Schulman once said. "I wish I had 12 Slick Wattses on my team."

Watts was a consistent bright spot over the next few years, but by

1977, many things had changed for the worse. Haywood, who had often

clashed with Coach Russell, was traded away. Other players on the team

had also grown tired of Russell's domineering coaching style.

JACK SIKMA

Finally, Schulman had seen enough; the owner forced Russell to resign in 1977. It was the end of an era in Seattle, but a more exciting one was about to begin.

{WILKENS RETURNS} Russell was replaced by Bob Hopkins, a former assistant coach. Unfortunately, Coach Hopkins couldn't stop the team's downward slide. Early in the 1977–78 season, the Sonics were an awful 5–17. Schulman then made another major change. He turned to

the team's new general manager—an old friend named Lenny Wilkens—

and asked him to take over as coach once again.

Wilkens accepted the offer and quickly reshaped

the lineup. He made Fred Brown the team's sixth man,

inserting high-scoring guard Gus Williams into the start-

ing lineup instead. Coach Wilkens also gave bigger roles

to Marvin Webster—a 7-foot-1 center known as the "Human Eraser" for

his shot-blocking skills—and sharpshooting rookie forward Jack Sikma.

Finally, Wilkens started young point guard Dennis Johnson in place of

Slick Watts.

Wilkens's "new" Sonics stunned the league by going 42–18 the rest

of the season, then roared through the playoffs to reach the NBA Finals.

"What did Wilkens have that Russell and Hopkins lacked?" asked Seattle

After his **1977** return, Coach Wilkens led Seattle to six winning seasons in seven years.

LENNY WILKENS

Steady guard Nate McMillan spent his entire 12-year NBA career with the SuperSonics.

sportswriter Blaine Johnson. "Maybe more organization, maybe more communication, [or] maybe he wound up with the right blend of per-

sonalities. One thing is certain—he put all the necessary ingredients into the pot at the right time."

In the Finals, Seattle faced off against the Washington Bullets, led by star center Wes Unseld. The series was an epic battle that began in Seattle's favor. The Sonics over-

came a 19-point deficit to win the first game 106–102. But after the teams split the next four games, things fell apart for the Sonics. Washington won by 35 points in game six, then held off a desperate Sonics comeback in the next game to win the championship.

Although disappointed, the Sonics vowed that they would be back, and they were. In fact, they faced off against the Bullets again in the 1979 NBA Finals. The Sonics weren't the same team, however. Webster

DENNIS JOHNSON

and Watts were gone, and Sikma had taken over as center. The forwards were Lonnie Shelton—the team's enforcer—and John Johnson. Williams and Dennis Johnson continued to form a magnificent guard duo, and

Fred Brown and Paul Silas provided great bench support.

Together, these players formed the "Seattle Seven," and they were

unstoppable in the Finals. The Sonics destroyed the Bullets four games to one, bringing Seattle its first NBA championship.

{STARS OF THE '80s} The Sonics had reached the peak of the

basketball world, but they would not stay there. Superstar

Magic Johnson helped the Lakers—the Sonics' main divi-

sion rival—rise to power, and many of Seattle's top players

soon moved on. Jack Sikma, the last remaining member

of the Seattle Seven, was finally traded away in 1986.

By that time, the Sonics were led by new coach Bernie Bickerstaff,

who had replaced Lenny Wilkens in 1985. Seattle was soon led by a new

collection of players as well. These included forwards Xavier McDaniel,

a skilled rebounder, and Tom Chambers, who led the team in scoring

and spectacular dunks. Guard Nate McMillan was the team's defensive

stopper, while Dale Ellis gave the Sonics lethal three-point shooting.

Also playing a major role was 6-foot-10 Derrick McKey, who was

ALTON LISTER

DALE ELLIS

so versatile that he spent time at all five positions during his rookie season with Seattle. "McKey has many gifts," marveled NBA analyst Rick Barry. "He can put it on the floor with either hand and tomahawk-dunk the finish, or he can hurt you with his turnaround jumper. He's also capable of flat-out shutting down his man on defense."

In 1988, Seattle added muscular power forward Michael Cage to its lineup. Cage was a dominant rebounder, especially on the offensive boards. With his help, the Sonics posted a winning record in 1988–89. But, as had been the case throughout the decade, the Sonics found little success in the playoffs.

{KEMP AND "THE GLOVE"} After missing the playoffs the next two seasons, Seattle brought in George Karl as its new head coach. Coach Karl believed he could rebuild the Sonics into a force.

"The X-Man," Xavier McDaniel, became a Sonics fan favorite with his rugged play.

25

XAVIER McDANIEL

Fortunately, he had inherited two rising stars who would help him do just that: forward Shawn Kemp and point guard Gary Payton.

Kemp had jumped directly from high school to the NBA, joining

the Sonics in 1989 at the age of 19. After a difficult first season, Kemp steadily improved as a scorer, rebounder, and defender. One area in which he needed little improvement, however, was dunking. With his long arms and explosive vertical leap, Kemp thrilled Seattle fans with an array of high-flying slams.

Payton had starred at Oregon State before being selected with the second pick in the 1990 NBA Draft. The wiry point guard quickly earned a reputation around the league for two things: tenacious defense and trash-talking. Payton was quick, but he was also incredibly strong for his size. Fans soon nicknamed him "the Glove," a reference to the way he tightly guarded his opponents.

Gary Payton led Seattle in the **'90s** with his unselfish offense and smothering defense.

Payton's aggressive, "in-your-face" style made him one of the NBA's most fiery competitors. In fact, he consistently ranked among the league leaders in technical fouls. Away from the court, however, Payton showed a softer side, staying active in the community and creating his own charity—the Gary Payton Foundation—to help underpriveleged children.

GARY PAYTON

By 1993–94, the Sonics were a powerhouse once again, finishing

the season with an NBA-best 63–19 record. Seattle's success was made

possible by such players as Detlef Schrempf and Sam

Perkins, intelligent veterans who were both deadly out-

side shooters. The main reason for Seattle's return to

glory, though, was the talented Payton-Kemp combina-

tion. "They've always been the two young guys," said

Coach Karl. "Now they've blossomed into perennial All-Stars."

Despite all their talent, the Sonics could never quite make it to the

top. No matter how great their regular-season record, they always

seemed to run into a better or hungrier playoff opponent. In 1995–96,

the Sonics powered their way to a 64–18 record and the Western

Conference title. Unfortunately, they then had to face the 72–10

Chicago Bulls in the NBA Finals. Although Seattle won two games, star

Guard Hersey Hawkins helped the SuperSonics lead the NBA in steals in **1995–96**.

HERSEY HAWKINS

guard Michael Jordan led Chicago to the championship.

{A NEW SONIC BOOM} By 1997, it appeared that the good

times in Seattle had come to an end. Feeling underpaid,

Shawn Kemp demanded to be traded. Although the

Sonics were disappointed to lose the five-time All-Star,

they were elated to acquire forward Vin Baker in return.

Baker had starred in Milwaukee the previous season,

In **1996–97**, Sam Perkins hit an NBA-record eight three-point-ers in one game without a miss.

averaging 21 points and 10 rebounds a game. Although Baker was not as

29

strong or spectacular as Kemp, he was a better passer and had a wider

assortment of moves. "What we've got from Vin is more versatility, clev-

erness, backdoor lobs, and spins," said Coach Karl. "There's more variety."

Baker teamed up with Payton to lead the Sonics to a 61–21 record

in 1997–98, but the changes continued in Seattle. Despite having led

the Sonics to seven straight winning seasons, Coach Karl was replaced

SAM PERKINS

The addition of shooting guard Ruben Patterson helped the Sonics fly high in **1999–00**.

RUBEN PATTERSON

Like Kemp before him, Rashard Lewis excelled at both scoring and shot blocking.

RASHARD LEWIS

by Paul Westphal, who would guide Seattle for two complete seasons.

After the team missed the playoffs the next year, many of the team's veterans were released and replaced by younger players such as guards Brent Barry and Ruben Patterson.

The Sonics, who were suddenly faster and more aggressive, returned to the playoffs in 1999–00. Leading the way was Payton, who enjoyed the best season of his career with 24 points and 9 assists per game. The Sonics also got a major boost from forward Rashard Lewis, who emerged as an explosive scorer.

In a little more than 30 years, the Sonics have captured one NBA championship and the loyalty of the Pacific Northwest. With this success have come growing expectations for another league title, a challenge Seattle is eager to meet. After all, no team knows more about flying high than the SuperSonics.

Seattle added size and experience in **2000–01** by trading for veteran center Patrick Ewing.

PATRICK EWING